Pythons and Boas

Pythons and Boas

Squeezing Snakes

Gloria G. Schlaepfer and Mary Lou Samuelson

Franklin Watts
A Division of Scholastic Inc.
New York • Toronto • London • Auckland • Sydney
Mexico City • New Delhi • Hong Kong
Danbury, Connecticut

Note to readers: Definitions for words in **bold** can be found in the Glossary at the back of this book.

Photographs © 2002: Animals Animals: 21 bottom (K. Atkinson/OSF), 6 (Joe McDonald), 37 (Raymond A. Mendez), 21 top (Allen Blake Sheldon); Art Resource, NY/Giraudon: 40; BBC Natural History Unit/E.A. Kuttapan: 38; Bruce Coleman Inc.: 5 left, 26, 27 (Cliff Frith), 30 bottom (John Giustina), 23 (Robert Weinreb); Corbis Images/D. Boone: 44; Gloria Schlaepfer: 13, 48, 49; National Geographic Image Collection/George Grall: 32; Peter Arnold Inc.: 20 (R. Andrew Odum), 12, 30 top (Gunter Ziesler); Photo Researchers, NY: 2 (Steve Cooper), 10 (Yoshiharu Sekino/PPS), 9, 28, 29 (Karl H. Switak); PhotoEdit/Michael Newman: 46; Visuals Unlimited: 16 (John D. Cunningham), 42, 43 (Ken Lucas), cover, 5 right, 11, 24 (Joe McDonald), 35 (Mary Ann McDonald), 34, 36 (Jim Merli), 14, 15 (David Wrobel).

The photograph on the cover shows a garden tree boa killing a bat in South America. The photograph opposite the title page shows a Solomon Island ground boa.

Library of Congress Cataloging-in-Publication Data

Schlaepfer, Gloria G.
    Pythons and boas : squeezing snakes / Gloria G. Schlaepfer and Mary Lou Samuelson.
        p. cm. — (Watts Library)
    Includes bibliographical references and index.
    Summary: Discusses the physical characteristics and behavior of various species of constrictor snakes, their relationship with humans, and how to keep one as a pet.
    ISBN 0-531-13954-9 (lib. bdg.)   0-531-16599-X (pbk.)
    1. Pythons—Juvenile literature. 2. Boa (Genus)—Juvenile literature. [1. Pythons. 2. Boa constrictor. 3. Snakes.] I. Samuelson, Mary Lou. II. Title. III. Series.
QL666.O63 S35 2002
597.96'7—dc21   2001005900

Contents

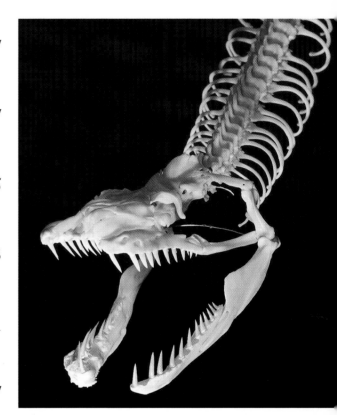

An emerald tree boa passes the afternoon in its rain forest habitat.

Chapter One

Pythons and Boas

Long tree branches droop in the water as a motorboat makes its way up the narrow river. The boat carries travelers exploring the Brazilian rain forest. The air is hot and steamy as the group stops to rest in a small clearing along the river's muddy bank. Bright rays of afternoon sun flicker through the thick layers of overhead leaves. Green vines curl around the trees' broad trunks. Some of the travelers walk into the forest. They brush against the leaves and vines.

Silently and smoothly, one of the vines begins to move. A woman catches sight of it and whispers to the others: "What is it?" With great excitement, they watch an emerald tree boa slide easily along a tree branch. The snake stops. Its body doubles and drapes around the limb like a gymnast on a horizontal bar. The snake's brilliant emerald-green back and yellow belly **camouflage** it among the leaves. "What a beauty!" exclaim the travelers as their cameras click. The snake slithers up into higher tree branches and disappears from sight.

A Special Name

Did you know there are twenty-five hundred different **species** of snakes in the world? Scientists divide them into **families**. The emerald tree boa, for example, is one species in a family of snakes called the Boidae (BOH-ih-dee). All ninety-five species of boas and pythons are included in the Boidae family. They share the special name **boids** (BOH-idz).

Boas are found on all continents except Australia and Antarctica. Pythons are found in Africa, Australia, and Asia, including the islands of Southeast Asia. Many boids make their homes in warm, wet tropical rain forests—their most common **habitat**. Some pythons and boas live in cooler climates, in dry sandy areas, or on rocky hillsides.

Members of the family Boidae come in all sizes. Some boid species are among the longest and heaviest snakes in the world. For example, the **reticulated** python can grow to a length of 30 feet (9 meters). That is as long as two medium-sized automobiles parked end to end. The largest and heaviest boa, the South American anaconda, may grow to a length of 33 feet (10 m)—a giant snake! In contrast, some dwarf ground boas found in the Antilles Islands are only about 12 inches (30 centimeters) long. Most boids, however, are medium-sized snakes.

The Hug of Death

Whatever their size, pythons and boas are **carnivores**, or meat eaters. Boids do not attack other animals with a poisonous bite as many snakes do. Instead they kill their **prey**—lizards, birds, rats, and other animals—by **constricting**, or squeezing, them to death.

Rudyard Kipling describes the boid well in *The Jungle Book:* "Kaa [the rock python] was not a poison snake . . . his strength lay in his hug, and when he had once lapped his huge coils around anybody there was no more to be said."

Imagine a boid is lying in wait, curled up on the forest floor, when a rat scampers by. Using its needle-sharp teeth, the

After seizing and killing a rat, this rainbow boa begins to swallow its prey.

Amazing Strength

Snakes, even small ones, are exceedingly strong. Once a squeezing snake starts wrapping itself around its prey, it is almost impossible to escape. Large anacondas have been known to kill and eat jaguars, caimans (pictured here), and even large crocodiles.

snake seizes and holds the wiggling **rodent**. Quickly, the boid winds its long, muscular body around its victim tighter and tighter until the trapped animal loses consciousness.

After the prey is dead, the boid relaxes. Since its teeth are made for grabbing and holding, not for chewing, the snake must slowly swallow its victim whole. How can a boid swallow an animal that is much larger and heavier than itself?

The jaws and necks of pythons and boas can stretch wide to engulf the body of a large animal. The snake's upper and lower jaws are separated into two parts that move independently from side to side. A bone connects the jaws like a hinge, so that the lower jaw can drop wide open.

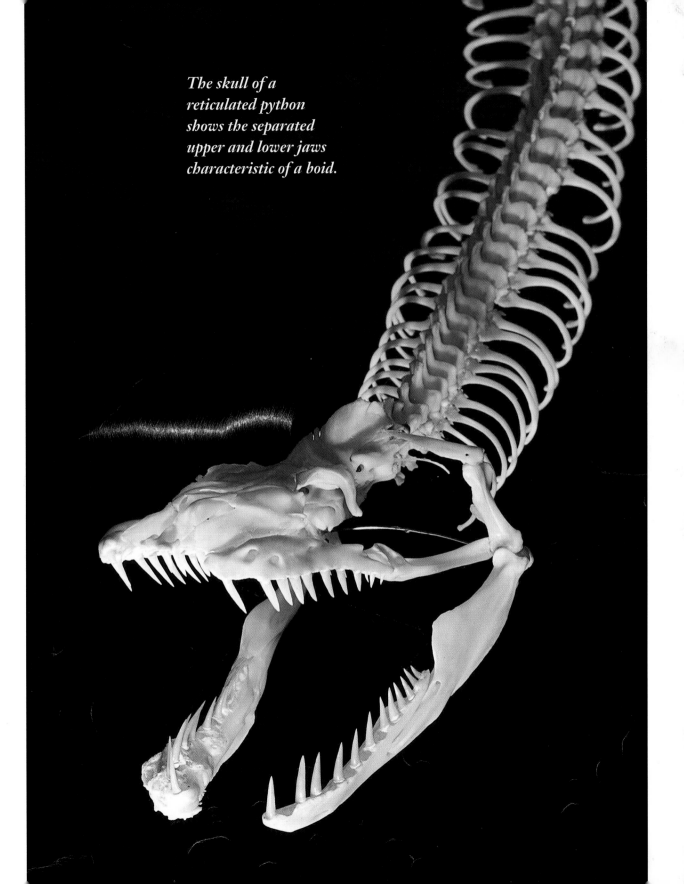

The skull of a reticulated python shows the separated upper and lower jaws characteristic of a boid.

Inching forward with its jaws, a rock python begins the long process of swallowing a Thomson's gazelle.

When the boid begins to eat, it grasps the victim's head with its curved teeth. Both the upper and lower jawbones on one side of its head reach forward, and the snake begins pulling its head over the prey. Then the jawbones on the other side grab hold of the creature's body and the snake's head moves farther forward. In this way, the dead animal moves down the snake's throat and into its stomach, a little bit at a time. If the meal is particularly large, swallowing might take many minutes.

Scaly Skin

A boid's elastic skin aids in swallowing because it stretches around the prey without tearing. Snake skin is composed of three layers: a clear, thin outer layer and two inner layers that are embedded with scales. Covering the body from head to tail, the scales are arranged in regular rows that form complex patterns. The snake's skin color, found in the bottom layer, shows through the first two layers.

Each boid species has its own colors and scale patterns. The scales around the mouth and eyes are usually large and irregular. On the snake's back, or **dorsal** surface, the scales are smaller, diamond-shaped, and sometimes overlapping. They are arranged side-by-side in rows. Across the snake's belly, wider, thicker **ventral** scales form single rows. Scales are

Every snake species has its own distinctive scale pattern. Shown here is a close-up of the body of a boa constrictor.

usually smooth and glossy, but on a few species, such as the rough-scaled sand boa, they are coarse and grainy.

Disguised Hunters

A boid's colors and scale patterns are not only handsome but also useful. The snake's skin provides camouflage that helps it blend into its surroundings. Thus, the vivid emerald green tree boa can move unseen through leafy trees in a tropical rain forest. A rosy boa's pale, brownish-pink color blends with the dry, rocky soil in southwestern deserts of the United States. In the woodlands of western North America, a rubber boa's shiny, chocolate-brown skin camouflages it among decaying logs and leaves. The striking colors and patterns of a reticulated python of Southeast Asia help it vanish into leaves and shadows.

The physical features of boids support their ability to be efficient **predators**, or hunters. Pythons and boas have an important place in the world's habitats. In the next chapter, we will take a closer look at these legless predators.

The rosy boa's scale pattern provides it with camouflage in the deserts of the southwestern United States.

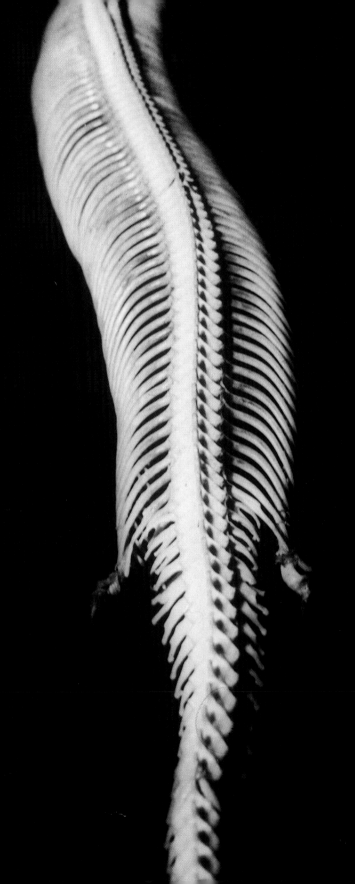

Snakes began to evolve from burrowing lizards during the Age of Reptiles, more than seventy million years ago. Pythons and boas still have small claws near their tails, as this python skeleton shows.

Chapter Two

Outside and Inside

Paleontologists believe that snakes **evolved** from burrowing lizards that lived underground. Dinosaurs were still roaming the Earth toward the end of the Age of **Reptiles**, more than seventy million years ago, when the lizards began to change. Slowly, over millions of years, their bodies evolved.

Over time, the lizards' visible outer ear decreased in size, until finally snakes had no outer ears at all. Eyelids also changed. Snakes now have a clear cap, or cover, over their eyes instead of eyelids. The limbs of these burrowing lizards also gradually grew smaller until they disappeared in many snake species. Primitive or less-evolved snakes, such as pythons and boas, still show traces of hind legs and feet—small claws can be found near the tail. Eventually, all snake species became sleek, streamlined animals—head, body, and tail.

Plenty of Bones

Snakes and humans have an important body characteristic in common: they are **vertebrates**, or animals with backbones. All vertebrates have a bony skull and a spine, or backbone, made up of many small bones. Humans have thirty-two or thirty-three bones in their spine. In comparison, a very large anaconda has hundreds of vertebrae. The spine provides support for the body. Without a backbone, a boid would be as limp as a cooked noodle.

Each bone in the spine is connected to a pair of curved bones called ribs. Together all the ribs form the rib cage. When a snake swallows a large meal, its rib cage expands. This allows the food to pass easily into the stomach. The spine extends into the snake's tail, but there are no ribs there. With its long, flexible spine, this legless animal can move sideways, forward, up, or down and can even swim. By counting the scales on a snake's belly, a person can learn how many bones are in the spine. There is one scale for each bone and its pair of ribs.

Hot and Cold

Snakes, lizards, turtles, tortoises, crocodiles, and alligators belong to a class of animals called reptiles. Reptiles are **ectotherms**, which means that their internal body temperature depends on the temperature of their surroundings. They get their body heat either directly from the rays of the Sun or from warm air, soil, or water.

Snakes need to stay warm in order to move, to digest food, to grow, and to reproduce. When they become cold, snakes warm up by basking in the sunshine or on a sun-warmed rock. If they get too hot, they cool down in the shade—in a hole in the ground, under a large rock, or in a clump of leaves. By moving back and forth between sun and shade, a snake can keep a constant internal temperature. This is why pythons and boas are most plentiful in warm, tropical habitats.

Senses for Survival

Snakes rely on several senses to tell them about their environment. Their sense of hearing is not one of those senses. Without external ears to direct sound waves, snakes are essentially deaf. Some sound vibrations do reach the inner ear by traveling along the jawbones. For instance, a ground-dwelling snake can detect heavy footsteps.

Boids have only a fair sense of vision. They can distinguish light from darkness but can detect movement only at close range. For example, imagine that a Cuban boa is following a scurrying mouse. If the mouse stops and sits still in the grass,

The Cuban boa relies on keen senses of smell and heat detection to track down its prey.

the boa might lose sight of it. If the snake had only eyes and ears, it would have a tough time hunting.

The boa can, however, use two well-developed senses to find the motionless rodent: its heat-detection ability and its sense of smell. Very sensitive pits on the face of the snake can detect the faint warmth of the little mouse. Like some other pythons and boas, the Cuban boa uses this sense to find warm-blooded prey or to hunt in dim light or darkness.

As the Cuban boa continues to follow the trail of the mouse, it also relies on a special sense. Continually flicking its forked tongue in and out, the boa senses the presence of the tiny mouse. The snake's tongue gathers chemical particles and carries them back to the Jacobson's organ, located near the nose. This organ "reads" the particles and sends a message to the boa's brain: mouse nearby! Quickly and gracefully, the Cuban boa slides across the ground to reach the mouse.

Learning with Their Tongues

Many people mistakenly believe that a snake uses its long, slender, forked tongue to inject poison.

The tongue actually functions to gather information about a snake's environment.

Sliding Snakes

It is remarkable that a snake can crawl, climb, or swim easily without the use of arms or legs. Snakes use several different methods of movement on land. Some travel in a **serpentine**, or wavelike, manner. Pressing against the ground, the snake

Pressing its body against the ground, an olive python moves in a serpentine manner.

moves forward in a series of S-curves. Its body and tail follow the same path made by its head and neck. Pythons and boas also use the serpentine movement to swim, or "crawl," in water. Snakes float because they hold air in their bodies.

Arboreal snakes, or snakes that live in trees, use the **concertina movement**. This action resembles the opening and closing of an accordion (also called a concertina). The boa's broad ventral scales, or **scutes**, anchor the front end of the snake's body to a tree branch. The rest of the body moves forward as much as possible in a series of loops. Next, the tail grips the tree branch and pushes the front end forward in accordion-like folds. Then the process repeats.

A giant snake like the Indian python moves with the caterpillar crawl. It uses its ribs, muscles, and scutes in this motion. The ribs act like legs, while the scales do the footwork. One group of muscles contracts, lifts up the ribs, and pulls the skin with its scutes forward. As another set of muscles contracts, the scutes are pulled down and back. The scutes work like the soles of athletic shoes by digging in and holding on to the ground. In smooth, rippling waves, the python inches along in a continuous straight line.

Scaly Bodies

A snake's scales are helpful in many ways besides helping it move. Scales protect the body from injury and from damage caused by rubbing against the ground or tree bark. They allow the snake to slide easily over many surfaces. The scales also prevent water from escaping through the snake's skin, so the animal stays hydrated.

As a snake increases in size, it outgrows its skin. Then the process of **molting** begins. First, the skin becomes dull and drab in appearance. Next, the transparent eye cap changes to a milky-blue color and becomes cloudy. At this point, the snake may hide for several days while its skin loosens.

When its eyes clear up again, the snake emerges from its hiding place. The old outer skin layer starts to peel off as the snake rubs its head and nose against rough rocks and roots. The skin around its mouth tears away first. While the snake crawls along the ground or through narrow places, its paperlike skin continues to shed. It turns inside out over the body, just as a T-shirt does when you pull it up over your head.

Molting occurs throughout a snake's life. When it is young and growing rapidly, a snake sheds its skin as often as seven times in one year. In adulthood, growth slows down, and molting is less frequent. After each molting, skin colors and patterns are bright and clear. Renewed with fresh skin and a big appetite, pythons and boas return to life as active and skillful hunters.

As a snake grows, it sheds its undersized skin regularly. The intergrade python pictured here has just finished shedding.

23

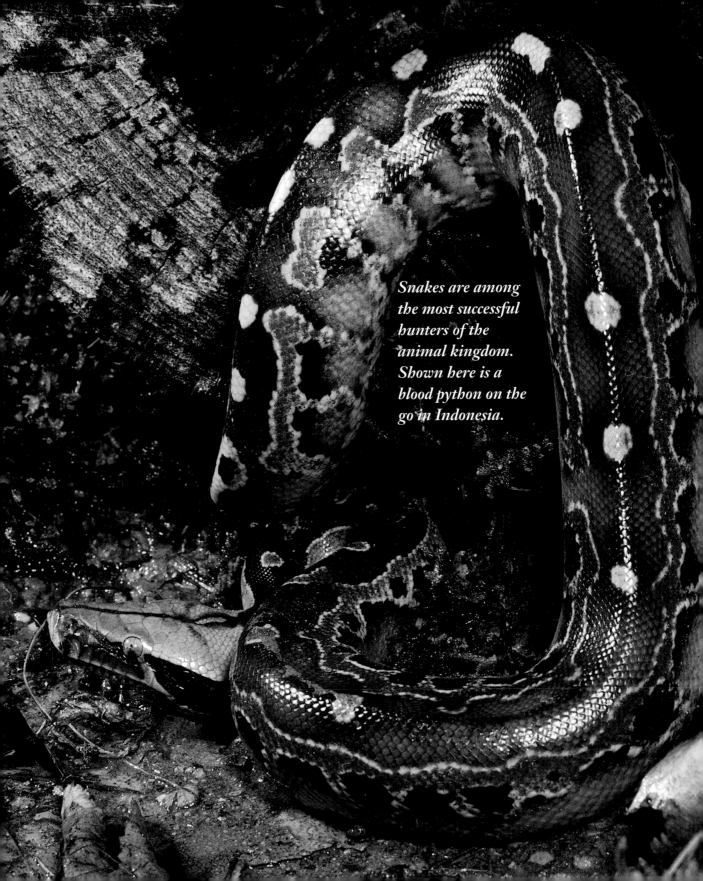

Snakes are among the most successful hunters of the animal kingdom. Shown here is a blood python on the go in Indonesia.

Chapter Three

Hidden Hunters

Snakes are solitary hunters. Their bodies move noiselessly through trees, on the ground, and in water. They pass easily through crevices, between rocks, and into small tree holes or underground **burrows**. Their protective covering makes them nearly invisible both to enemies and to potential prey. Snakes cannot jump, fly, or run; they cannot grab with talons or claws; nor do they hunt in packs. Yet snakes are superb hunters and successful survivors in a variety of habitats.

A Varied Menu

Catching and eating animals, or **predation**, is a snake's most important and time-consuming activity. What a boid catches depends on its size, its habitat, and the other kinds of animals that live in its world. Lizards, birds, and rodents are the mainstay of a boid's diet. Snakes are opportunistic, however; they catch and eat any size animal they can swallow.

Young and slender boids devour animals such as mice and small lizards. The tiny Australian pygmy python is one example. The pygmy never grows longer than 2 feet (0.6 m). This petite python, which lives in termite mounds, eats the little **geckos** that feast on the termites.

Large boids catch and swallow a great variety of prey. Mammals, lizards, and ground-dwelling birds make up most of their diet. The huge scrub python, found in the Australian coastal rain forests, can grow to 13 feet (4 m) long. It eats opossums, fruit bats, bandicoots, birds, and lizards. This python was reported to have killed and eaten a 50-pound (23-kilogram) kangaroo! Such a large meal has its drawbacks, however, because the python becomes swollen and can move only with great difficulty. In that condition, even a big python is vulnerable to predators.

Mimicking a Poisonous Snake

Pacific boas are known as mimics of the death adder because they defend themselves just as the adders do. When threatened, they hiss and strike out from a coiled position to frighten an enemy away.

Catching Meals

The vivid green tree python of New Guinea is an arboreal snake that seldom leaves its dense tree habitat. This tree-bound boid is also a successful hunter. It uses its strong **prehensile** tail like a hand to grasp and hold tightly on to a branch. From there it dangles and strikes out at rodents, birds, and even bats. Sometimes a young green tree python lies in wait and wiggles its tail to attract prey—usually frogs and lizards.

Ready to strike at any moment, a green tree python holds tightly on to a branch with its tail.

An Indian sand boa escapes from the heat—and awaits lizards and rodents—under a cover of sand.

A different kind of hunter lives in hot, dry, scrubby areas of India, Pakistan, and Afghanistan. The small, tan Indian sand boa hides from the day's heat under rocks or a light cover of sand. Only its head is exposed. In some species of sand boas, the eyes point upward, such that the snake is able to see while partially buried in sand. When a lizard or rodent comes near, the boa bursts from the sand and quickly seizes it. The snake then coils itself tightly around the prey's body until the victim becomes unconscious.

A Desert Struggle

Despite its small size—less than 2 feet (0.6 m) long—the sand boa is able to defend itself against its chief enemy, the desert monitor lizard. When a monitor catches a boa, the snake wraps around the lizard's neck and squeezes tightly. As the monitor loses consciousness, it releases the sand boa.

Another burrowing snake, the medium-sized Calabar ground python of West Africa, tunnels under leaves on the forest floor or crawls into rodent burrows in search of prey. This python's head and tail are both black and rounded. When it is alarmed, the snake presses its head to the ground and winds its body into a ball, protecting its head. The python's thick tail is raised, so it looks like the snake's head. By waving its tail back and forth, this boid confuses its enemy.

Potential enemies have a hard time making heads or tails of the Calabar ground python!

The Infamous Anaconda

Perhaps the best known of all the boas, the heavy-bodied anaconda is the largest snake in the western hemisphere. This giant lurks mainly in swamps and sluggish rivers in tropical

South America. It moves effortlessly in water. Similar to a crocodile, its nostrils are on top of its snout so that it can breathe easily as it swims.

As the anaconda waits in shallow, murky water, only its eyes and nose are visible. Swiftly it strikes at birds, turtles, frogs, or any small mammal that passes. Dr. Harry W. Greene, an expert on snakes at Cornell University, gives a vivid example of an anaconda's effect on the surrounding animals: "Tamarins often crossed the edge of a Peruvian lake on fallen tree trunks, until a green anaconda, hidden by **aquatic** vegetation, struck from below and ate one. The surviving tamarins avoided that route for days, and perhaps their descendants still chatter nervously when approaching the water."

This anaconda's head is barely visible above the water as it lurks in the tropics of Brazil.

Even birds—such as the egret pictured here—are vulnerable to the powerful anaconda.

Large anacondas are capable of killing and eating wild caimans, boars, and jaguars. Such a meal satisfies the boa, and it may sleep for days. Months may pass before it eats again.

Hunting Strategies

Pythons and boas catch their food in two ways: passively or aggressively. Most boids sit and wait, lying quietly in a place where prey animals move around. The boid's camouflage and ability to remain motionless make this strategy very effective. A lizard, rodent, or bird scurrying nearby does not see the quiet snake. One swift strike, and the prey is caught.

A few boid species are more active hunters. Quickly they follow their prey or flush out small animals from tree branches, rock, or shrubs. They might try several times before catching a meal.

Occasionally, stories are told about giant pythons or boas attacking and eating people. It is true that large boids have killed people. **Herpetologists** (scientists who study reptiles and amphibians) and experienced reptile hunters say that such attacks are rare, however. Giant snakes generally do not see humans as a meal.

Threatened Species

Even its great size and strength cannot protect the anaconda from its greatest enemy: humans. The snake is threatened with **extinction** by destruction of its forest habitats. Large anacondas are also hunted for their beautiful and valuable skins.

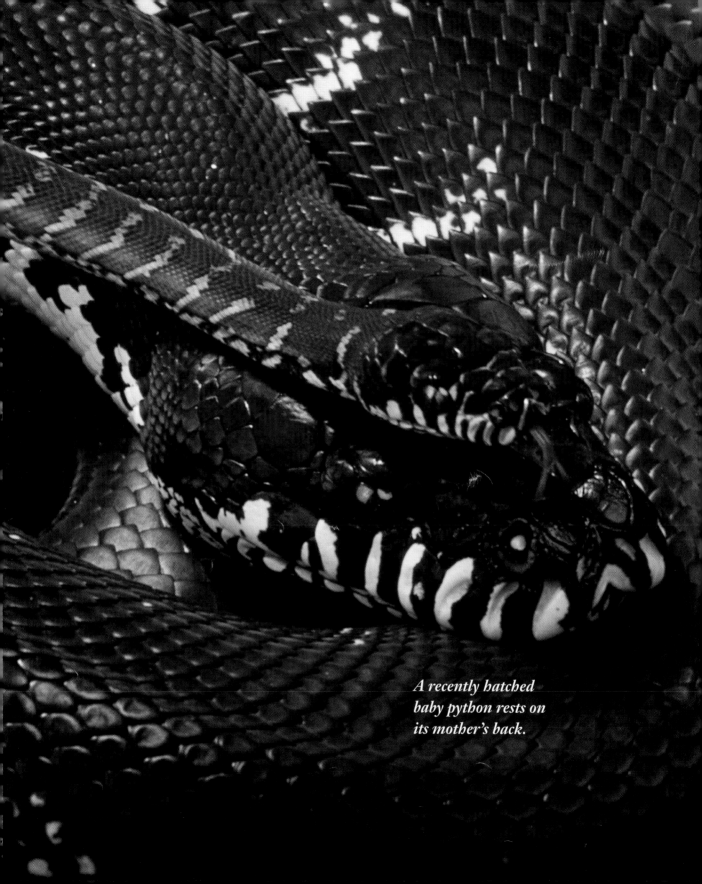

*A recently hatched
baby python rests on
its mother's back.*

Chapter Four

A New Generation

At least once a year, male pythons and boas seek out females in order to mate. Four to nine months later, the young boids emerge. Pythons and boas reproduce differently. Pythons are egg layers, while boas give birth to fully formed young snakes.

Hatching Pythons

The number of eggs laid by a female python varies according to species. For example, the Angolan python deposits a small **clutch** of four to five eggs, while other species lay a dozen or more eggs. Indian, African, and reticulated pythons lay thirty to sixty eggs and occasionally produce up to one hundred.

A mother python seeks out a protected, damp, warm spot under rocks or in a pile of rotting leaves. With her body, she scoops out a small pit in which to lay her eggs. Python eggs are oval shaped and have a tough, leathery shell. They are slightly sticky when laid, and this causes them to **adhere** to each other.

Unlike most egg-laying snakes, the female python stays with her clutch of eggs and protects them. She coils her long body around the piled eggs and rests her head on top of them.

Some python species, such as the Burmese, incubate their eggs by constantly twitching their muscles.

Burmese python hatchlings take a first look at the world and each other.

Egg Facts

Unlike chicken eggs, snake eggs change in size and shape. During incubation, the eggs absorb moisture from their surroundings and become lumpy as the young snake develops inside.

She leaves the nest only to drink water. Some of the larger python species, such as the Indian and the Burmese, actually **incubate** their eggs. By constantly twitching their muscles, these pythons raise their body temperature and keep the eggs warm. A consistently warm temperature during incubation ensures that more eggs will develop and hatch. This is a remarkable feat for an ectotherm.

After two or three months, the mother python's job is finished. The **hatchling** uses its egg tooth—a sharp, pointed cutting tooth—to slash several openings in the tough shell. It takes anywhere from a few hours to more than a day for the young snake to emerge through the broken shell.

A rough-scaled sand boa gives birth to several babies.

Boa Babies

Boas do not lay eggs. After boas mate, the developing **embryos**, or unborn snakes, grow within egg sacs inside the mother's body. **Gestation**, the time of an embryo's growth, ranges from 100 to 200 days, depending on the species. When the young boas are ready to be born, the mother boa pushes the sacs out, and the baby boas break free.

Whether born or hatched, most baby boids look and behave like small copies of their parents. A few species, however, have distinctly different skin colors. A green tree python, for example, can be either yellow or brick-red upon hatching. As it grows, its colors change to the adult's bright green.

Growth Spurts

Only 17 to 20 inches (43 to 50 cm) in length at birth, boa constrictors grow quickly. After a few months, they reach 36 inches (91 cm). In two to three years, when they are mature, boa constrictors measure 6 to 10 feet (1.8 to 3 m). Then they continue to grow more slowly.

Soon after birth, young boids look for food. They know by **instinct** how to hunt. Juvenile pythons and boas grow rapidly, shedding their skins seven times or more during their first year of life.

Obstacles to Survival

Many types of **parasites** make their homes in the bodies of young snakes. Most wild snakes have external parasites on their skin. Ticks and mites adhere to the skin and suck blood from the host snake. These external parasites are spread by contact between snakes or are picked up from plants on the ground.

Boids get internal parasites from the food they eat. When a python or boa eats an animal that has tapeworms, the snake becomes a new host for the parasites. Several species of

The tick is a common parasite that plagues many boids. Here, a tick prepares to feed on the blood of a python.

The hunter has become the hunted. A tiger makes a meal out of a python in India.

worms—flukes, roundworms, and tapeworms, as well as single-celled animals called **protozoa**—live within the bodies of snakes. Although parasites are common among boids, they are rarely fatal.

A young boid does have its share of fatal enemies, however. As soon as a boid is born or hatched, it becomes potential food for another animal. Large water beetles, big spiders, and even other snakes make quick work of slim young boids. Even as they grow larger, pythons and boas have enemies waiting for them, such as large lizards or crocodiles. Wild, carnivorous mammals such as ocelots, tigers, civets, mongooses, and pigs include snakes in their diet. **Feral cats** (abandoned pets) also kill snakes. Birds of all kinds enjoy a good snake meal, too. Long-billed egrets and herons, Australian kookaburras, and sharp-eyed secretary birds are expert snake catchers that snap up boids and swallow them whole. Even boids as long as 3 feet (1 m) are not safe from the strong talons of birds of prey such as red-tailed hawks and serpent eagles.

Snake Defense

With so many natural enemies, a boid's best defense is concealment. Quiet and secretive, the snake simply does not call attention to itself. Its long shape and protective coloration help it to disappear into its surroundings.

When confronted by an enemy, however, a boid does act to defend itself. It might coil into a tight ball, protecting its vulnerable neck and head from injury. It might raise its body and hiss at the foe. Many attack with a painful bite. Others slither or swim away as quickly as possible. Boids have little defense, though, against humans—the greatest destroyers of snakes.

A Painful Lesson

Snakes' tails do not **regenerate,** as their relatives the lizards' do. If a predator grabs and bites off a snake's tail, the snake lives the rest of its life with the stub or shortened tail end. It never grows back.

Through the years, human cultures have viewed snakes with fear, awe, reverence, and disgust. This Aztec manuscript depicts a man being eaten by a snake.

los q̃ nacion a qui o̅ra
de hombres Ricos

Chapter Five

Pythons, Boas, and People

Over the centuries, human cultures have had different attitudes toward snakes. Early humans believed that wild animals gave them special hunting power. Their cave paintings depicted snakes along with other important animals such as bison, horses, and deer. In ancient Greece and Rome, people observed snakes shedding their skins. To these societies, snakes became symbols of eternal youth, healing, and rebirth.

Cultural Beliefs

Some ancient peoples protected and worshiped animals, including snakes, as gods. For example, people of the Mayan and Aztec cultures made hundreds of giant stone carvings that portrayed snakes, including the feathered Aztec serpent-god Quetzalcoatl. Python worship also was common in western and central Africa. Harming the sacred boid was considered a serious crime punishable by death. Today, in parts of Asia, people believe that an albino, or white, python brings good health and fortune.

Snakes have a much more negative role in Christian traditions. For example, in the biblical story of Adam and Eve, the snake is portrayed as an evil creature. Feelings of fear and disgust toward snakes in North American society might stem partly from that portrayal.

Snakes are not evil, however. They play an important role in the natural world by controlling rodent populations. Humans benefit from this because mice and rats eat grains and other crops.

A Greek Myth

Greek myths include a story about a giant snake called Python. It terrorized villages until it was slain by the Greek god Apollo.

Humans kill snakes for use in many types of leather goods. These golf shoes are made from illegally hunted python skin.

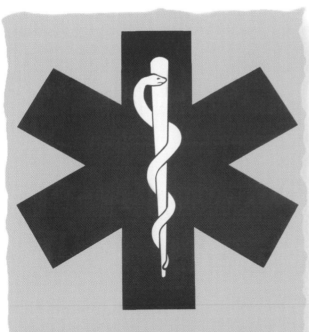

Caduceus, Symbol of Healing

In ancient Greece, Asclepius, the Greek god of healing, was pictured holding a walking stick with a snake entwined around it. This image developed into the symbol for physicians. It is called a caduceus.

Rodents may also carry harmful diseases such as hanta virus and plague. Many people are unaware of these benefits, and snakes continue to be killed in great numbers. Their beautiful skins are used for making shoes, boots, and other leather goods.

Boid Business

Buying and selling reptiles is a big business. Every year, 1 to 2 million live reptiles are removed from their habitats and taken to the United States for the pet trade. The recent popular interest in unusual pets, such as Indian pythons, is one reason that the animals are **endangered**, or threatened with extinction, in the wild.

Because many pythons and boas are endangered, their collection and trade are regulated. Under a 1975 international agreement called the Convention on International Trade in Endangered Species (CITES), Indian pythons, Argentine boa constrictors, and Madagascar boas may not be sold at all. Trade in all the other species in the Boidae family is strictly regulated to prevent these snakes from becoming rare.

Habitat Loss

More snakes are lost through habitat destruction than through any other means. The steady increase in the world's human population causes many changes in the environment. Trees in tropical and temperate forests are cut down. Marshlands are drained and filled with dirt, and grasslands and deserts are plowed and graded. In their place, roads crisscross the landscape, and homes and towns appear. Farms sprawl over land that was once wild, and oil wells and mines dot the landscape. Snakes and other creatures cannot survive the dramatic change in their habitats. They have nowhere to live.

People are beginning to realize the importance of preserving large portions of natural land. They are trying to balance human needs with those of plants and animals. Through the efforts of these **conservationists**, people around the world are becoming more aware and concerned. As a result, the animals that live in natural habitats—pythons and boas included—might have a place to live for many more generations.

One good place to learn about boids up close is the nearest zoo. Here, a zookeeper does a demonstration with a boa constrictor.

Chapter Six

Pythons and Boas As Pets

A zoo is the best place to see and learn about pythons and boas, including some unusual and rare species. Today, many snakes exhibited in zoos are **captive-bred**, meaning they are not taken from the wild. Zookeepers are specially trained to care for snakes and to provide an environment that comes as close as possible to their wild habitats.

After a visit to a zoo, you might become interested in a pet python or boa. If this happens, it is important to ask for advice and information. First, check to see if your city has any laws or rules about keeping snakes as pets. Knowledgeable experts, either in person or through books, magazines, or the Internet, can answer questions about buying a boid and building a cage or terrarium. They can also help with species selection, kinds of food, feeding schedules, temperature requirements, handling safety, growth and shedding, and caring for a sick pet.

When choosing a pet, look for a clean, disease-free snake. Examine it for external parasites such as mites, which are found between scales and around the eyes. Mites are tiny parasites that suck blood. They multiply quickly and can eventually kill the snake. Mites can also carry and transmit an incurable disease called inclusion body disease (IBD). Nontoxic sprays and powders can control these parasites.

It is also important to observe the snake's gums by carefully pulling back its lips. Infected places in the mouth and on the jaws are a sign of mouth rot. This condition is a fairly common but treatable disease in pythons and boas.

If you decide to get a pet boid, be sure to obtain one that has been captive-bred. In that way, you will help conserve pythons and boas in their natural habitats. If you have a genuine interest in these remarkable reptiles, a pet python or boa can provide a fascinating and fun learning experience.

Keeping a Pet Boid Healthy

To keep a small python or boa safe and in good health, you need a simple screen-topped terrarium. The top must fit securely so that the snake cannot push it up and escape. A 20-gallon (76-liter) tank is adequate for small snakes. A heat source must be properly located to maintain the correct temperature and to prevent burns to the animal. It is best not to heat the entire tank, so the boid can move to a cool area when necessary. Most snakes tend to hide occasionally, so put a large

Because they are small and even-tempered, ball pythons are among the best boid species to keep as a pet.

stone, branch, or piece of bark in the tank. The main idea is to make the snake feel comfortable in its environment.

Brent Williams, a reptile specialist from California, suggests that first-time owners obtain small boid species—ideally a ball python, rosy boa, or red-tailed boa. Says Williams, "I don't recommend larger snakes like the reticulated pythons or anacondas. They're too big and unpredictable."

Many parents worry about snakes biting. Patricia Peña, a boid owner, says, "Most animals can nip when scared, and a snake is no exception." Some pythons and boas quickly become tame and are easily handled, but others, such as reticulated pythons and African rock pythons, can be nervous and irritable all their lives. Also remember that a cute little baby snake might someday become truly immense!

Mealtime

Feeding is another common concern. Knowing what and when to feed a pet boid calls for experience and common sense. Young snakes eat often; adult boids usually need food once every three to four weeks.

Williams recommends prekilled food if the snake will accept it. Feeding live rats or mice to a snake can be a challenge. If the boid is not hungry and does not attack its prey within 20 minutes, the live food should be removed. This prevents possible biting injuries to the snake. Surprisingly, a pet snake will not always defend itself, and it has no means of escape.

Lots of Choices

Small pythons and boas may accept lizards as food for a couple of months. Packaged or frozen foods for snakes are sold in pet stores, by telephone, and through the Internet.

Caring for a Pet Boid

- Expect to take full responsibility for the care of a boid. It's your pet.
- Get as much information as you can before making a decision to buy a boid.
- Find others who share your interest and who already have boids.
- Choose a species that is known to be even-tempered and is recommended by an expert.
- Inquire about and provide an adequately sized cage and heating source, properly located.
- Use sterilized or treated bedding. Keep the snake's home clean to prevent disease.
- Wash your hands before and after feeding your boid. Reptiles may carry salmonella bacteria that cause disease in humans.
- Have an adult with you when you are feeding or handling your pet.
- Provide your snake with water in a dish.
- Learn about the kind of food your pet eats and needs. Buy the food from a reliable source.
- Provide vitamin and mineral supplements to help your pet grow strong and to prevent disease.

Glossary

adhere—to stick or hold fast

aquatic—taking place in or on water

arboreal—living in trees

boid—a snake that is a member of the Boidae family; a python or a boa

burrow—a hole in the ground made by an animal for shelter

camouflage—coloring that hides something or someone by making it look like its surroundings

captive-bred—produced and raised in captivity by breeders

carnivore—a plant or animal that eats other animals

clutch—a group of eggs

concertina movement—the accordion-like movement of some snakes

conservationist—one who helps to save or to protect natural resources, including wildlife

constrict—to squeeze

dorsal—on or near the back

ectotherm—an animal whose body heat comes from an external source, such as the Sun

embryo—a developing animal before birth or hatching

endangered—nearly extinct

evolve—to change and develop gradually over time

extinction—a state of nonexistence

family—a group of related species of organisms

feral cat—a cat that has escaped from domesticity and become wild

gecko—a nocturnal, insect-eating lizard

gestation—the time during which a female animal carries developing young within her body

habitat—the area in which a plant or animal lives

hatchling—a newly hatched animal

herpetologist—a scientist who studies reptiles and amphibians

incubate—to keep eggs warm for the purpose of hatching

instinct—a natural, pre-programmed behavior

molt—to shed hair, feathers, or skin and grow a new covering

paleontologist—a scientist who studies past geological periods using fossil remains

parasite—an organism that feeds and lives on, or in, another organism

predation—the act of preying on other animals

predator—an animal that hunts other animals for food

prehensile—flexible, used for grasping and seizing

prey—an animal hunted by other animals for food

protozoa—microscopic, single-celled animals

regenerate—to replace a body part through the growth of new tissue

reptile—one of a class of vertebrates that includes alligators, crocodiles, lizards, snakes, and turtles

reticulated—having a pattern like a network or a web

rodent—a small gnawing mammal, such as a mouse or a rat

scute—an external plate or large scale

serpentine—winding back and forth in an **S** shape

species—a group of organisms with many common characteristics. These organisms can mate and have offspring.

ventral—on or near the abdomen or belly

vertebrate—an organism that has a backbone

To Find Out More

Books

Barth, Kelly L. *Snakes*. San Diego: Lucent Books, 2001.

Burton, Dr. Maurice, and Robert Burton, eds. *International Wildlife Encyclopedia*, 3rd edition. New York: Marshall Cavedish, 2002.

Cooper, Paulette. *277 Secrets Your Snake Wants You to Know*. Berkeley, CA: Ten Speed Press, 1999.

Ling, Mary, and Mary Atkinson. *The Snake Book*. New York: DK Publishing, 1997.

Mehrtens, John M. *Living Snakes of the World in Color*. New York: Sterling Publishing, 1987.

Simon, Seymour. *Snakes*. New York: HarperCollins
  Publishing, 1992.

Videos

Land of the Anaconda. National Geographic Video, 1998.

Nightmares of Nature: Deadly Reptiles. National Geographic
  Video, 1997.

Organizations and Online Sites

Defenders of Wildlife
1101 14th Street NW #1400
Washington, D.C. 20005
http://www.defenders.org/index.html
This organization is dedicated to the protection of all native
wild animals and plants in their natural environments.

National Wildlife Federation
11100 Wildlife Center Drive
Reston, VA 20190-5362
http://www.nwf.org
This organization promotes environmental education and the
conservation of natural resources.

Reptiles Magazine
http://www.animalnetwork.com/reptiles/

Sierra Club
85 Second Street, Second Floor
San Francisco, CA 94105-3441
http://www.sierraclub.org/
The Sierra Club promotes conservation of the natural environment by influencing public policy decisions.

Smithsonian Institute
National Zoo/Reptile Discovery Center
http://www.natzoo.si.edu
This site provides information and photos about the animals found in the zoo.

A Note on Sources

Our research began in the library, where, after consulting with a reference librarian, we read many books for young readers. Then we searched for general information about pythons and boas in standard reference works, such as the *Animal Life Encyclopedia, Reptiles,* by Dr. H. C. Bernhard Grzimek. Next, we moved on to more specialized references. Chris Mattison's *Snakes of the World* and Clifford H. Pope's *Giant Snakes* were very helpful. The magazine *Reptiles* provided useful current information as well as colorful photographs. The Internet was also an important source.

Whenever possible, we observed pythons and boas first-hand. We enjoyed visiting schools with Brent Williams, a reptile specialist, who let children see, touch, and interact with his pythons and boas in the classroom.

We are often asked, "How do two people write together?" We do not divide up the work, but rather devote our time together to research, write, rewrite, and edit our manuscript, sentence by sentence. After trial and error, we have found that this is the system that works best for us.

The authors wish to thank Brent Williams for sharing his knowledge and interest in reptiles, as well as Dr. Harry W. Greene for reviewing the manuscript.

—Gloria G. Schlaepfer and Mary Lou Samuelson

Index

Numbers in *italics* indicate illustrations.

photos of, *11*, *16*, *21*, *24*, *27*, *29*, *34*, *35*, *49*
skeleton, *16*

Quetzalcoatl, 42

Rain forest, 7–8, 14
Regenerate, 39, 55
Reptile, 17, 19, 31, 44, 55
Reticulated python, 8, *11*, 12, 14, 34, 50, 55
skull of, *11*, 12
Ribs, 18, 22
Rodent, 9, 20, 26, 27, 28, 29, 31, 44, 55

Scales, 13, 18, 22–23, 48
Scute, 22, 55

Senses for survival, 19–20
Serpentine, 21–22, 55
Size, 8–9, 26, 28, 36, 39
Skin, 13–14, 22–23, 31, 44
human use for, 31, 44
Sliding snakes, 21–22
Smelling sense, 20
Species, definition of, 8, 55

Tail, *16*, 18, 27, 29, 39
Tick, *37*, 37
Tongue, 20, 21

Ventral, 13, 22, 55
Vertebrate, 18, 55

Williams, Brent, 50

About the Authors

Gloria G. Schlaepfer has a master of science degree in environmental studies. She shares her love and respect for the natural world through her writings, photography, and community activism. In 1997, she received the Clara Barton Spectrum Award from the Red Cross for her volunteer work on behalf of conservation and the environment. Schlaepfer, who lives in California with her husband Karl, has four children and four grandchildren.

A graduate of Dominican University in Illinois, Mary Lou Samuelson earned two teaching credentials at California State University, Fullerton. While teaching reading and language arts, she was a member of the California Literature Project. She enjoys sharing the art of writing with schoolchildren, as well as with her ten grandchildren. She lives in Fullerton, California, with her husband, a college administrator.